WARSAW

"Cities, and big cities in particular, might be said to mirror the societies which erect them; conversely, the myths that are born as cities are built in turn shape the societies. Day-to-day reality may seem to contradict this view. When considered in isolation from their times, houses, streets or passers-by may appear ordinary, normal, undistinguished. But a moment's reflection, a penetrating look probing life around us will reveal to us the genius of history. Then every cobble will resonate with echoes of history, dawn will light up every window, wind will puff up the white clouds gliding slowly along the grey river and a dome of blue will appear above the city."

Paweł Hertz, *The Myth of Warsaw*

WARSAW

Text by Piotr Rafalski

Photographs by Jan Morek

Translated by Karol Jakubowicz

Interpress · Warsaw · 1986

Designed by Jerzy Kępkiewicz

ISBN 83-223-2248-8

It all began long before the city's first buildings appeared on the escarpment towering over the Vistula with two roads intersecting near a ford. As long as 1500 years ago, one of these roads — today known simply as international motorway E-70 — served merchants travelling with their caravans from the South of Europe — as a route to the Baltic shore. There, they bought amber, much beloved of elegant Roman ladies. In time, a fortress was built on the Vistula to protect the ford. We have practically no information on what it looked like. Well over seven centuries ago, in 1262, the warlike tribe of the Samogitians overran it and burnt it down. It was a bitter defeat. Prince Ziemowit I, the ruler of Mazovia (or Mazowsze the Polish name for that part of the country) was killed in battle. His 11-year old son, Conrad was captured.

So, a search began for a more easily defensible place, where a new fortress could be built. It was found about two miles due North, where there was another ford. A town began to spring up around the fortress. It was named Warsaw.

Just when that happened, nobody can tell precisely. The town's charter has perished. Elsewhere, a big fuss might be made about it, but in Warsaw... Varsovians have always been rather happy-go-lucky, carefree, informal folk, treating documents with healthy irreverence. From their point of view the legend about the beautiful but pugnacious Mermaid who helped establish the town and is now on its coat of arms, does entirely satisfactory service as the official history of Warsaw's origins.

Over seven centuries have passed since then and much water has flowed under the bridges that eventually came to span the Vistula. The city has grown, spread, come up in the world and serves the nation in ever new ways. One thing, however, has remained unchanged: Poland's capital lies right in the centre of the European continent, at the crossing point of many trans-European highways. Just look at the map. Motorway E-7 from Rome and Vienna meets here with road E-8 from London through Rotterdam, Berlin and on to Moscow, and road E-81 meets in Warsaw with motorway E-12 from Leningrad to Prague, Nuremberg and Paris.

The first detailed description we have of the town comes from the early 14th century. To explain why it came to be written, we have to go back in time almost a hundred years. In 1226, Prince Conrad of Mazovia appealed to the Teutonic Knights to defend his principality against the Prussians. Having conquered Prussia, the Teutonic Knights turned against Poland and overran Pomerania, Kujawy and the Dobrzyń region, leading to a series of wars with Poland. King Casimir the Great appealed to the Holy See to adjudicate in the conflict. In consequence, the nuncios Galhard de Chartres and Pierre, canon of Annécy, arrived in Warsaw from Avignon, as representatives of Pope Benedict XII. Warsaw was not exactly world-famous then, and the Pope wanted to be sure that the Papal Tribunal could meet there for a session. The nuncios' recommendation was favourable to Warsaw and so on 4 February 1339, the Tribunal was convened in the house of Bartłomiej, the *wójt* (King's representative, serving as mayor) of Warsaw, in the Market Square. The verdict was read out at the Church of St. John the Baptist on 15 September of that year. The Papal Tribunal ruled in favour of Poland, ordering the Teutonic Knights immediately and completely to restore to King Casimir the Pomeranian, Kujawy and Dobrzyń regions, previously overrun by them by force of arms. The Knights never did restore any land unless they absolutely had to, but historians agree that the verdict was a great moral triumph for Poland. Fortunately, when that particular conflict again came to a head in 1410 during the battle of Grunwald, the Poles added a resounding military triumph to the earlier moral one.

The records of the proceedings of that trial include many valuable documents, but none is more interesting for historians of Warsaw that the report of the papal nuncios. They wrote that Warsaw was encircled by defence walls, that it housed the Prince's residence, as well as three churches and "an abundance of inns, taverns and whatever else a traveller may require"; finally that "access to the town [was] safe and easy". An accurate and favourable opinion, perhaps even too accurate and detailed in places. His Holiness Benedict XII must have found his patience and sense of humour wearing thin as he read that "there is also a parish school in Warsaw". And yet, God bless you, reverend fathers, for including that bit of information in your report. It gives us an objective yardstick to gauge the cultural distance between the capital, Cracow (where as early as 1364 a university — the second oldest in Central Europe — was founded), and Warsaw, where the existence of a "parish school" was something to write home about — quite literally in this case. At that time there was absolutely nothing to suggest that the little Mazovian town would one day rival Cracow as *totius Poloniae urbs celeberrima*. But let us be patient. Two centuries later a series of events began to turn into reality what had seemed unimaginable during the reign of Casimir the Great.

To begin with, the last two descendants of the Mazovian Piast dynasty, Princes Stanisław and Janusz, died suddenly, leaving no progeny. Their beautiful Renaissance-style tomb of Chęciny marble can be seen in St. John's Cathedral in Warsaw. In consequence, the Mazovian Parliament on 10 September 1526 swore an oath of allegiance to the Polish King Sigismund I. By the same token, the era of Mazovia's autonomy came to an end. After the King's death, his estates in Mazovia were inherited by his widow, Queen Bona. In 1550, she moved from Cracow to Warsaw together with her three daughters, Sophia, Anne and Catherine. There are those who will say that she does not count as a Varsovienne, because she spent only seven years in Warsaw and then returned to her native Bari in Italy (where she died a year later). Such carping would be typical, because surely few people in Polish history could have had as bad a "press" as Queen Bona. Still, it is only fair to recall that during her few years in Warsaw, that elderly woman succeeded in pushing through several much-needed reforms, including the establishment of an early form of fire insurance. When she planted her vegetable garden on the escarpment at Ujazdów, Varsovians derided her efforts to change the unhealthy Polish diet by introducing Italian vegetables into the country. They called vegetables "that Italian stuff" and delighted in saying: "Let Italians eat lettuce, a Pole who eats it can but starve to death". And yet, today no self-respecting Polish housewife would dream of starting dinner without a plentiful supply of "that Italian stuff".

After Queen Bona's departure for Italy, two of her daughters, descendants of the Jagiellonian dynasty, stayed behind in Warsaw: Anne, the future wife of King Stephen Báthory, and Catherine, soon to marry John III Vasa, the future King of Sweden. The story of their love, marriage and the events surrounding it, inspired many writers, from Marcin Kromer in the 16th century (*The True Story of the Pitiful Adventure of the Finnish Prince John and the Polish Princess Catherine*) to the 20th-century Finnish poet Eino Leino (*The Songs of Prince John and Catherine of the Jagiellons*). We will return to this story later on, for John and Catherine bore a son, named Sigismund after his grandfather and uncle, who became a King of Poland.

Meanwhile, however, in 1569 the Polish Seym met in Lublin to proclaim the union of Poland and Lithuania. It decided, among other things, that the Seym of the Commonwealth of Two Nations would thereafter meet in Warsaw. That decision immediately set in motion major construction projects in the city. In that same year, the outstanding Italian architect, Giovanni Battista Quadro (who had designed the Renaissance town hall in Poznań) set to work on reconstructing the old castle of the Mazovian Princes. It was to house the Seym, but also — and this is important — to serve as the King's residence. Sigismund Augustus, the King of Poland, never returned to Cracow and the Wawel Castle, from the Lublin Seym. He decided to move the capital to Warsaw.

And so, looms in Brussels, Antwerp and Brugge started producing tapestries ordered by Sigismund Augustus for the Royal Castle in Warsaw. Also, work began on a project which inextricably tied the last of the Jagiellons with Warsaw's history: the construction of a bridge over the Vistula. That bridge can be seen on the oldest panorama of Warsaw, known as *Braun's Panorama*. F. M. Sobieszczański writes: "Georg Braun, i.e. Brunus, was the dean of the collegiate church *in gradibus* in Cologne at the turn of the 16th and 17th centuries. Together with Francis Hogenberg he published in the years

1592—1618 *Civitates orbis terrarum in aes incisae et excusae descriptione topographica, morali et politica illustratae* in 6 volumes in folio with plates depicting the major towns of Europe". A description of Warsaw was included in Volume IV *Theatri praecipuarum totius mundi urbium*, Cologne 1618.

Here is what Braun wrote about that bridge: "Sigismund Augustus has had a wooden bridge built across the Vistula. It is 1150 feet in length and arouses widespread amazement and admiration. Its length and beauty are hardly surpassed by those of any other bridge in Europe." Well, it's ironic to think that today's publishers complain about the time it takes for a book to appear. When Braun's book was being brought out by the Cologne publisher in 1618, the bridge had been nothing but a memory for 15 years, having been swept away by a spring flood in 1603.

After Sigismund Augustus' death, Kings Henry Valois and Stephen Báthory continued to rule the country from Cracow. But Sigismund III Vasa, the son of Catherine the Jagiellon and John III Vasa we mentioned before, transferred the capital and his court and government to Warsaw. Some Cracovians will argue that the move was prompted by the King's poor health ("The King was sickly and the doctors recommended that he lead a country life, and that is why he left the capital and moved to Warsaw"). Be that as it may, the 400th anniversary of that event will soon be upon us. We are beginning to glance at the calendar with some anxiety: will the first line of the Warsaw Underground be ready for the anniversary?

In its first years as the capital, Warsaw extended its area to over 300 acres and was ringed by a new line of earthworks, fortified with bastions (the so-called Sigismund Line). New, foreign-sounding names were added to the list of builders of Warsaw, beside architects Giovanni Battista from Venice and Giovanni Quadro who had worked in the Jagiellonian period. They were Giovanni Trevano (who continued the reconstruction of the Royal Castle and built the King's private residence, the Ujazdów Palace), Constantino Tencalla, Agostino Locci and many others. Up until the 20th century, many generations of Italian architects would use their talents in the service of Warsaw; many would choose to remain in Poland, regarding it as their second homeland.

In the first flush of excitement after Warsaw was made the capital, six monumental aristocratic residences were built in the city, as well as about 60 manor houses in outlying areas around Warsaw. In the mid-17th century, the city had 18,000 inhabitants.

A Swedish invasion, known in Poland as the Deluge, put an abrupt stop to that period of fast growth. It was the culmination of a period of Polish-Swedish hostilities extending over 60 years. Poles spent more than half of the 17th century on horseback, fighting wars with Sweden. That period was full with moments of both triumph, and shameful defeat. Anyone wanting to know what it was all about should take a look at the plaque mounted on the Western side of the plinth of the Sigismund Column in Warsaw. It reads: "Sigismund III, King of Poland by virtue of free elections, King of Sweden by virtue of inheritance, succession and right." Improbable, yes, but largely speaking that is what the whole Vasa period was about: the Polish Vasa kings had not given up their claim to succession to the Swedish throne and were determined to impose on the Swedish Protestants the very creed they did not want: Catholicism. The Polish-Swedish wars have their literary record in *Potop* (*The Deluge*) by Henryk Sienkiewicz, one of the best-loved books of several generations of Poles. It also gave birth to an extensive body of literature jotted down on the spot by the men who fought them: Wespazjan Kochowski, Jan Chryzostom Pasek and Erik Dahlberg, a Swedish general, the author of the most beautiful panorama of Warsaw "before the Deluge" and of panoramas and views of other Polish towns. He kept a diary during the fighting and wrote towards the end: "So, the Polish war, in which His Majesty the King fought personally, is over for the time being. All of us who have come through safely cannot thank the Almighty enough for His gracious protection and for letting us survive such great danger." So wrote an old hand at soldiering, a veteran of many campaigns, who clearly knew what he was talking about. It was a fierce war, a juggernaught which rolled across Poland,

and particularly Warsaw, with a destructive force equal almost to that of the Second World War. Warsaw's population fell from 18,000 to 6,000, that is by proportionately as much as during the war of 1939—45. 80 per cent of buildings along Krakowskie Przedmieście lay in ruins. So did most of those along Długa, Trębacka, Świętojerska and Nalewki Streets. Some areas of Warsaw, like Powiśle and Grzybów, were completely devastated, with just a few buildings left standing. Praga, on the Eastern bank of the Vistula, was the scene of three days of pitched fighting and was gutted. It is precisely that district of Warsaw which today boasts a Swedish Street. There, too, traces of that battle of three centuries ago are still to be seen. Mention of them can be found in a poem by Władysław Syrokomla, a 19th-century Warsaw poet:

> ...A Swedish rampart and several graves along the coast
> painful witnesses of the times of King John Casimir...

Even today, as one drives northward along the Eastern bank of the Vistula, past Saska Kępa, a small iron cross can be seen on the dyke, just about opposite the old airfield of Gocław. If you look closely, you'll find an inscription on it confirming that it marks one of the graves mentioned by Syrokomla. And if from that spot you look across the river towards the centre of the town, you will not fail to notice skyscrapers towering over the town's panorama, built in the 1970s by the Swedish companies BPA and Skanska Cement. General Erik J. Dahlberg, who after the Polish campaign was so grateful to the Almighty for his miraculous rescue, would be greatly surprised to know that centuries later Varsovians would name a street after him. All that is past history, passions are all spent, quarrels forgotten, and yet *The Deluge*, written a century ago and dealing with Polish-Swedish wars, is still alive in us, the incurable optimists of Warsaw. It was to us that Henryk Sienkiewicz addressed its message, expressed pithily in the final toast proposed by Zagłoba: "Should hard times befall our country again, let our countrymen remember us and never despair, for no straits are so desperate that they cannot *viribus unitis* with God's help be overcome."

The years 1660—85, a quarter-century of hard work to raise the city from the ashes left behind by the Swedish invaders, is a period of Warsaw's history particularly close to the hearts of those of us who have done their share to reconstruct Warsaw after the Second World War. Varsovians had a hard time of it already then. In May 1660, peace was finally signed in the refectory of the Cistercian monastery at Oliwa, after 60 years of incessant strife, and King John Casimir graciously deigned to renounce his family's traditional claim to the Swedish throne of the Vasas. War continued in the Eastern regions of the country, but Warsaw, in the centre, could finally breathe more freely and reconstruction could begin. Much like architects Pniewski and Gutt after the Second World War, so in that epoch Tylman of Gameren and Agostino Locci spearheaded Warsaw's reconstruction. The list of Tylman's work is very extensive, to mention but the palaces of the Krasińskis and of the Ostrogskis, the Bernardine Church in the Czerniaków district and the church of the Sacramentalist sisters in the New Town Market Square, or Marieville (built where the Opera House stands today and destroyed 150 years ago), at once a hotel and the city's commercial centre. Agostino Locci may have fewer illustrious buildings to his credit, but it is enough to mention one to suggest the quality of his achievement: Wilanów, King John III's (Sobieski) private residence, and as fine an example of the architect's craft as could be found anywhere.

It was to Wilanów that envoys of the Emperor of Austria made their way in the hot summer of 1683 to ask King John III to come to the rescue of Vienna, then besieged by the Turks. Tradition has it that they found him in the orchard, tasting the first of a bumper crop of plums. As a matter of fact, plums do not ripen in Poland before September, but let us not split hairs. The story is very much in character, because after the rigours of wartime, King John III enjoyed withdrawing to his estate, to listen to the rustling of bulrushes, or of the poplars he himself had planted along the bank of the Vistula, and to pick fruit in his own orchard.

The Austrian envoys begged the King personally to come to the rescue of Vienna at the head of his army. The King was ready to assist the Austrians, but pleaded infirmity (at 54, he was not so young as he had been), asking to be excused from going to war himself. He extolled the military prowess of his commanders, Jabłonowski and Sieniawski. In the end, however, he yielded to entreaties, mounted his horse, and — sitting in a high, Turkish-style saddle — led his army against the Infidel. What happened then is common knowledge. In 1983, Poland and Austria celebrated the 300th anniversary of the lifting of the siege of Vienna and the rout of the Turks. Two votive churches still standing in Warsaw commemorate those events, the Capuchin Church in Miodowa Street, built by Locci, and the church of the Sacramentalist sisters in the New Town Market founded by Queen Marie Casimire, built by Tylman of Gameren. King John III's Palace in Wilanów, extended by its successive owners in the 18th and 19th centuries, is visited every year by thousands of tourists from around the world. Our own generation, too, has added to its magnificence: in 1968, the reconstructed 19th-century riding school was turned into the Museum of Posters, these being the *specialité de la maison* (as French-born Queen Marie Casimire might have called them) of Poland's contemporary art.

If the ups and downs of Warsaw history were presented in a diagram, it would look very much like the temperature chart of a malaria patient. From its peaks, representing the moments of the town's greatest glory and prosperity, the line tumbles immediately into the nether regions, symbolic of gloom and despair. And so, after the dazzling victory in the battle of Vienna, there followed the Great Northern War (1700—21) against Sweden and the gloom of the Saxon era, the most depressing period in the history of the Republic and its capital. Sodom and Gomorrah! Howewer, while no righteous men could be found in the biblical Sodom and Gomorrah, some people in Warsaw did labour mightily to banish evil and promote virtue. Let us pick out two of them, as different as night and day in terms of rank, temperament and character. Their portraits are on display in the Historical Museum of Warsaw and it is clear that they looked different, too. One was Franciszek Bieliński, depicted as wearing a wig and an embroidered coat decorated with the star of the Order of the White Eagle. His likeness brings to mind an azalea, a georgeous, proud azalea. The other is Father Pierre G. Baudouin. In this portrait, painted in his later years, his face inescapably reminds one of that childhood treat, a baked apple.

Franciszek Bieliński was the Crown Marshal, the highest-ranking official in the Republic. He was austere, uncompromising, overbearing. His contemporaries cannot have been too fond of him, as he was always imposing new taxes, and always wanted more money. He headed the Komisja Brukowa (Street Commission), initiating and supervising its projects. They were certainly needed and important, but he can have been under no illusion that they would go down in history as grand achievements. Quite simply, he had streets paved, swamps drained, canals dug, and organized Warsaw's original sanitation department. Bieliński wanted to drum cleanliness into the Varsovians and was far from lenient with the slovenly ones. He commissioned Pierre Ricaud de Tirregaille, architect *civilis et militaris*, to compile a *plan de la ville de Varsovie*. Completed in 1762, it was a work of rare beauty. Some authorities claim that the map was dedicated to Franciszek Bieliński. Not so. The dedication, to be found at the bottom on the left hand side, is addressed to King Augustus III. Bieliński's name can be found on it, too: he was the man who had commissioned it, and who paid out the sum of 2,533 zlotys and 10 groszys to M. de Tirregaille. It was a considerable amount of money, but M. de Tirregaille had earned it fully, as his map of Warsaw was the first one based on precise measurements. It shows that Warsaw had streets like Goworka, Bartłomieja, or Queen Aldona, but not a Franciszek Bieliński Street. Such a street is not to be found on a contemporary map, either. Some would say that the name of Marszałkowska (Marshal) Street harks back to the times of Marshal Bieliński and his work. True, he had planned it himself, and it was named after his office. But still, that is modest recognition of his work — although, admittedly — very much in his own style.

Compared to the stern and despotic Bieliński, Father Pierre Boudouin was a paragon of goodness and sweetness, a real saint who — but for someone's oversight — should have been canonized a long time ago. He was born in Avesnes, France, and lived long and virtuously. He came to Poland to take up an appointment as confessor to the holy orders of the Sisters of Charity and Nuns of the Visitation, brought over to Poland by Queen Marie Louise. Soon, however, it transpired that this would be virtually a sideline, compared to his main work. Father Baudouin's heart was in care for children, for homeless orphans of whom there were so many in war-ravaged Warsaw. Soon, his lodgings were full of little urchins. The lodgings proved much too small for them all. A whole house had to be rented to accommodate them. Soon it, too, was overcrowded. The French philanthropist displayed great initiative and organizing talent. He won support for his venture among influential people and appealed to the generosity of Varsovians. He organized many collections and raffles. Finally (thanks no doubt to behind-the-scenes manoeuvring by Father Pierre) recipients of orders and medals bestowed by the King were put under an obligation to pay a regular sum of money for charity. Professor Andrzej Zahorski, a historian who is an authority on that period of Poland's history, has written on the subject: "It was not easy to get those noblemen to pay up. Until the end of the Republic, hospital authorities needed great ingenuity and strength of purpose to get some of the back overdue payments out of magnate's coffers: full to bursting, but jealously guarded". 1762 saw the completion of Father Pierre Baudouin's lifetime work: the construction of the Son of God Hospital. Because of its size it was also known as the General Hospital and it had 1000 beds. Just think what dogged perseverance and dauntless refusal to take "no" for an answer were needed to wangle, beg and extort the money for such a hospital, completed six years before Father Pierre's death.

Historical sources give us no indication that Marshal Bieliński and Father Pierre Baudouin ever met, but then Warsaw had no more than 60,000 inhabitants at the time and their paths must have crossed one way or another. Certainly the great nobleman would not have made friends with the humble missionary, and on the other hand Father Pierre would have found the Crown Marshal too peremptory and high-minded for his liking. We do know that Pierre Baudouin was in contact and worked together with Józef Załuski (founder of the famous Załuski Library) and Stanisław Konarski, the Piarist who organized the Collegium Nobilium. It was in Konarski's honour that King Stanislaus Augustus had a medal struck with the legend *Sapere auso. Sapere auso!* — all the righteous men of the Saxon Sodom and Gomorrah should have been companions of this order. It was they who infused Poland with the spirit of Enlightenment during the final years of the Republic and even after the partitions.

Among the buildings erected in Warsaw in the first half of the 18th century were several palaces (Pałac pod Blachą, the Mniszech and Blue Palaces, the Branicki Palace). Then, there was the so-called Saxon Axis, a town-planning venture of considerable scope, initiated by King Augustus II, continued for thirty years and never really finished. It called for creating a string of squares, gardens and buildings along an East-West axis. Only some parts of it are left today: Victory Square, for several decades now the object of town-planning studies and competitions meant to complete it according to some carefully thought-out plan; the Saxon Garden, reduced in size in the late 1940s, when the Marszałkowska Street already mentioned above was extended northwards; and a part of the old barracks of the Royal Guard which within living memory has always housed the 4th Station of the Fire Brigade. Not much is left of the Saxon Axis on the ground, but it has been preserved in the memory of Varsovians, tradition and in the names of new buildings erected along its length. For example, we know nothing of the gallantry on the battlefield of General Wilhelm Mier, commander of a regiment of the Crown Guard (we do know that he died in his bed in 1758), yet his name lives until today. The 4th Station of the Fire Brigade is known as the Mirowski Station. A trade emporium built nearby in the 19th century is known as Hala Mirowska. The nearby housing estate is known as Mirów. The same is true of the Plac Za Żelazną Bramą (Behind the Iron Gate Square). The Iron Gate, built as part of the Saxon Axis, was dismantled as early as 1818. Yet, a housing estate built on the site in the 1960s and 1970s was named the Iron Gate Estate. No trace is left of the Saxon Palace, blown up by the Nazis after the Warsaw Rising in 1944, nor of pavilions built in the Saxon Garden by Dresden architects Pöppelmann and Jauch. Nonetheless, some Varsovians can still point to the spot where an open-work pavilion, known as the grand salon, stood in the Garden. From there fat and in-famous King Augustus II "hunted" dogs driven by servants straight before the muzzle of his rifle.

In the Age of Enlightenment, Warsaw grew in stature as a centre of science, art and culture. 1773 saw the establishment in Warsaw of the Commission of National Education, the world's first Ministry of Education. The first secular school, the Cadet School, training men for the Corps of Cadets established by King Stanislaus Augustus (Poniatowski), educated its students to be enlightened citizens. Some of them, like Tadeusz Kościuszko, a national hero of both Poland and the United States, were soon to be catapulted to fame by the turn Polish history was taking.

Towards the end of the 18th century, Baroque was replaced in Warsaw architecture by a local variety of classicism, known as the "Stanislaus style", after King Stani-slaus Augustus. And indeed his influence can be seen in construction work done in Warsaw at the time: in his private residence, in the Łazienki Park, and in the recon-struction of the interior of the Royal Castle.

For such reasons, if not for others, the reign of King Stanislaus Augustus can be recognized as a happy time in Warsaw's history:

> ...The town assumed a new shape and it almost seemed
> that Warsaw marvelled greatly at itself...

as the poet Adam Naruszewicz wrote in somewhat affected tones. We are very fortunate that a magnificent pictorial record of what Warsaw looked like then has come down to our times. It is a collection of 26 paintings by Bernard Bellotto, also known as Canaletto.

Before coming to Warsaw, Canaletto was the court painter of Augustus, Elector of Saxony (later elected King of Poland), for whom he had painted seventeen landscapes showing the most important views of Dresden, the capital of Saxony. The outbreak of the Seven Years' War (1756—63) and the King's death in 1763 ended the Dresden period of Canaletto's life. He had to look for a new patron. On the advice of another painter, Stefano Torelli, who found employment at the court of Catherine II, he set off with his family in 1767 for St. Petersburg. On his way he stopped over for two days in Warsaw to visit a painter friend, Marcello Bacciarelli... And that was it: Warsaw cast its spell on him and he was to spend the rest of his life in Poland's capital, devoting his work, his life and his love to it. He arrived in Warsaw in the third year of the reign of King Stanislaus Augustus and one of his paintings depicts the King's election on the fields of Wola. It shows an extensive plain crowded with joyful, happy people, cheering and jubilating. Cannon boom, horsemen gallop to and fro, while long ranks of cavalry units of the *levée en masse* of the gentry stretch far into the background. Nowhere to be seen, however, is the main hero of the occasion. Canaletto portrayed His Majesty the King in another painting. He is shown as observing Canaletto himself at work on one of the main achievements of his oeuvre: *A General View of Warsaw Seen from Praga*.

Canaletto takes us in his paintings along the streets of Warsaw in the 1770s. It was a time when Warsaw could temporarily breathe freely and again many buildings were going up everywhere. So, many of the buildings in Canaletto's paintings are sur-rounded by scaffolding, showing that they were just being erected, or renovated. Cana-letto was a realist, and if shacks and lean-tos stood cheek by jowl with magnificent magnate residences, he would include both in his painting. He faithfully recorded street scenes, showing people of different rank and position passing one another in the street. And again we see contrasts in his paintings, with opulent riches rubbing shoulders with poverty and utter misery. In short, what we have here is a dispassionate, painstakingly precise portrayal of what Warsaw looked like during the reign of King Stanislaus Augustus. So, as has been said, Canaletto was a realist. True, but with some exceptions. Take the sky over Warsaw: in his paintings it is always bright blue, and usually cloudless. Now, statistically speaking, it rains in Warsaw for an average of 156 days, and it snows for an additional 56 days in the year. So could the sky have really looked like that all the time? Certainly not. One is tempted to say that the sky was "imported", a recreation of the sky of his childhood on that Venetian lagoon where this Varsovian "by choice" had been born.

Hair-splitting specialists also point to some other inaccuracies to be found in Canaletto's landscapes, e.g. the fact that the Northern wall of the Palace of Princess Lubomirska in Mokotów (which today houses the Warsaw Musical Society) is bathed in abundant sunshine, a rather unlikely occurrence at Warsaw's geographical latitude. But then, Canaletto — great craftsman that he was — cannot simply have made a mistake. If love makes the world go round, could not his love for Warsaw have shifted the Palace around a little, so that he could "see" the sun shining directly on its Northern wall?

On 3 May 1791, the Polish Parliament, sitting in session at the Royal Castle, adopted a Constitution. It was the world's second constitution after that of the United States adopted in 1787, and the first in Europe, a few months ahead of the French one. Historians note that few of the potential opponents of the Constitution were present. The session was called immediately after the Easter recess and they had not yet returned from their estates. Moreover, Varsovians in their thousands crowded by the Castle and in its courtyard, eying the opponents of the draft Constitution "with unmistakable hostility". And so, the Constitution of the Third of May, as it has come to be known, was passed, to be acclaimed by many in Europe (particularly in revolutionary France) and in the United States. It could not, however, reverse the tide of history and save Poland, by then a weak country long corroded by anarchy. Its fate was sealed by the expansionist, rapacious policies of the three neighbouring powers: Russia, Prussia and Austria. Despite the heroic National Rising of 1794, led by Tadeusz Kościuszko, Poland was partitioned and lost her independence for over 120 years.

The last moments of Stanislaus Augustus as King of Poland are described by a biographer thus: "On 7 January 1795, Stanislaus Augustus left Warsaw on the order of the Russian authorities and set out for ... Grodno, the place of his exile. And suddenly, the common people of Warsaw, the mob that several months earlier had wanted to hang him, showed its love and grief for the King. Thousands, tens of thousands of men, women and children ran by his coach and crowded between the horses of the Russian dragoons accompanying the King, wringing their hands, tearing their hair out, weeping and lamenting. After so many years as King of Poland, it was the first and only time that Stanislaus Augustus saw tears of love for him streaming down the faces of thousands of people. But by then it was no more than a way of bidding farewell to the last King of Poland, and to the country's independence."

As has already been said, Varsovians are informal folk with little reverence for official documents. So, after King Sigismund III Vasa moved from Cracow to Warsaw in 1596, Warsaw was known as "the capital". Formally speaking, however, it was nothing of the sort. It was "the residential town of His Majesty the King". But now the last Polish King has left Warsaw under escort to abdicate in Grodno. The Royal Castle became the seat of foreign governors or viceroys. By spearheading the national liberation struggle of the Polish people, Warsaw reaffirmed and reinforced its moral right to be the capital of the country. It became a symbol of Poland's history, independence strivings and the nation's unity.

The short period of the Napoleonic wars, and of the Duchy of Warsaw in the years 1807—15, fuelled great expectations among the Polish people, ending in equally great disappointment. If you ever find your way to the courtyard of the Pałac pod Blachą, remember that it was the scene of a beautiful and moving event, when on Christmas Day 1812, General Stanisław Potocki, the last (fifth!) commander of the Polish Corps of Napoleon's Grand Army brought his rag-tag group of survivors from the war before the Commander-in-Chief of the Duchy of Warsaw's Army, Prince Józef Poniatowski. The exhausted men in tatters had dragged 40 cannon with them almost literally on their backs — all that was left of the corps' artillery. To comfort their Commander-in-Chief, they showed him the eagles on the pennants of no-longer existing regiments. An eye-witness reported that "Prince Józef was in tears and could not bring himself to utter a single word".

Vain hopes lay shattered after Napoleon's defeat. The Congress of Vienna in 1815 created the Congress Kingdom of Poland, linked by a personal union to Russia. While ruled by a Russian viceroy, it initially had its own Parliament, government and army. After the November Rising of 1830—31, that semblance of independence was curtailed, and after the January Rising of 1863—64, it was wholly abolished.

Tourists looking for what is left of 19th-century Warsaw usually tour such sights as the Opera House, the Staszic Palace, or a classicist complex built before 1830 by Antonio Corazzi and today housing the Town Hall at what is known as Dzierżyński Square. They are also taken to see churches incorporating in their design certain features of historically Polish styles, e.g. the St. Stanislaus Church in Wola and the St. Florian Church in Praga, both designed by Józef P. Dziekoński. The tour also takes in the building of the Society for the Encouragement of the Arts, designed by Stefan Szyller. Still, the climate of 19th-century Warsaw is most authentically preserved in the red-brick walls of Praga factories, in the Russian-built citadel and in some buildings of the industrial district of Wola. They are among the few surviving remnants of that "Age of steam and electricity" which increased the city's population tenfold — from 63,000 in 1800 to 686,000 in 1900. On the map of 19th-century Europe, Warsaw was an industrial centre of some importance. The first factories were built in districts, like Powiśle, close to the Vistula river, to take advantage of cheap river transport. It was there, too, in a factory belonging the Lilpop-Rau-Loewenstein partnership, that Ludwik Waryński, the founder of Poland's first working-class party, was launched on his revolutionary career. In addition to machines and technologies, other things, too, were brought in from the industrialized countries of Western Europe, including the slogan *Proletarier aller Länder, vereinigt euch!* was soon translated into Polish.

When the first railway line reached Warsaw in the mid-19th century, it facilitated the growth of industry in the Wola and Praga districts. The construction of the railway station of the Warsaw-Vienna line at the intersection of Jerozolimskie Avenue and Marszałkowska St. was another milestone in the city's development in the 19th century. The centre of the town shifted to the vicinity of the station and the development of Southern districts began.

The administrative borders of Warsaw remained unchanged since the 18th century. The city's growth was hindered by the Citadel in the North, built in reprisal for the November Rising of 1830—31, and a ring of forts built around the city in the 1880s. In the late 19th century Warsaw was one of the most overcrowded cities of Europe. In many areas just North of the city centre, the population density was over 1,500 people per hectare of land. It was then, towards the end of the 19th century, that a famous Frenchman, Ferdinand de Lesseps, predicted a brilliant career for Warsaw — a city located in the very centre of the continent — as Europe's largest metropolis (and that at a time when the population of only eight cities of the world exceeded the one million mark). That prediction was to fascinate Varsovians for a long time. In 1911, Lesseps' undoubted authority was additionally reinforced by the appearance of Henryk Sienkiewicz's novel for young people *W pustyni i w puszczy* (*In Desert and Wilderness*). It deals with the African adventures of Staś Tarkowski, whose father was employed on the construction site of the Suez Canal. So, people would say, somewhat naively, perhaps: "Lesseps? Why, that's the boss of Mr. Tarkowski, father of Staś, the brave little boy whose adventures are so beautifully described by Sienkiewicz. Well, if Lesseps says so, then certainly he knows what he is talking about." Almost a hundred years on, ever new generations of young people read of the adventures of Staś, and Ferdinand de Lesseps' prediction has yet to come true. Mindful of the crises plaguing the great metropolises of the world, we say "Thank God for that".

The distinguished reporter Olgierd Budrewicz, who has made writing about Warsaw his speciality, once wrote: "Warsaw is a small town, a small town of a million inhabitants." Today Warsaw has 1,640,000 inhabitants, but it is still medium-sized as European capitals go. Despite all the shortcomings and deficiencies and everyday troubles, life is most probably easier in Warsaw than in one of the huge megalopolises, ever growing in number.

No doubt this goes partly to the credit of Polish town-planners who have spent the last 70 years working to prevent the catastrophe of over-extensive growth. In 1915, after retreating Russian troops had blown up bridges on the Vistula behind them, Warsaw was occupied the very next day by troops of the 9th Army of Prince Leopold of Bavaria. The new invaders proved no less tough than the previous ones, but the changing vicissitudes of the First World War prompted them to seek some accommodation with the Poles. Warsaw was put under Polish local government which immediately incorporated the suburbs into the capital, extending its area from 34.1 to 115 square kilometres. Warsaw Polytechnic was re-polonized and a Faculty of Architecture was established. It included a Chair of Town Planning held by the eminent town planner, Professor Tadeusz Tołwiński. The professor also headed a team of Polish architects which embarked on preparing Warsaw's first modern development plan under the modest title *Preliminary Sketch of the Regulation Plan of the Capital City, Warsaw*. The team took just half a year, between June and December 1916, to complete it. It was pioneering work, calling for, among other things: extension of Marszałkowska Street northwards towards Żoliborz; construction of a new North-South thoroughfare parallelling Marszałkowska Street; extension of Jerozolimskie Avenue towards the Grochów district; and linking railway lines encircling Warsaw by means of a tunnel cutting across the city centre. The plan introduced for the first time the concept of "airing corridors": "Wooded urban areas, whether in the form of parks or gardens, or broad avenues, should cut like wedges towards the centre of the city, broadening towards the suburbs and finally linking up with forests or fields outside the city." For the first time, too, the idea of a Warsaw underground (Metropolitain as it was then called) was mooted in that plan. It envisaged that Wola and Praga should be set aside as industrial districts and Żerań turned into a big inland river port. In conclusion, the authors, with enviable modesty again, stressed the preliminary nature of their plan, and urged the creation of a special office charged with continuing the town-planning work they had begun. And indeed, 1917 saw the establishment of an Office for Regulation and Town Settlement. It is in that Office that today's Bureau for Planning the Development of Warsaw has its roots; this is a large establishment of over four hundred town planners, architects, specialists in various fields of municipal life, economists, sociologists, and geographers. They have their work cut out, coping with the difficult problems of a growing city and the surrounding area, but still, if need be, are capable of sending specialists, individually, or in whole groups, to other cities needing help, like the earthquake-shattered Skopje in 1963, Lima, Damascus, Nicosia and many others. And it all started with the *Preliminary Sketch of the Regulation Plan of the Capital City, Warsaw* of 1916.

As has been said, during the time of partitions Warsaw was universally recognized by Poles as their capital, and the capital of their country, Poland. In November 1918, as the First World War drew to a close, small Polish army units, supported by students and scouts, disarmed the German garrison. Warsaw was at long last free of occupying forces, free to assume for good the role of the capital of a reborn Polish state. Its path was strewn with many obstacles, however, arising out of 120 years of foreign rule, retarded growth and the invaders' deliberate policy of holding back development. On top of that, there was war-time destruction to cope with — in Warsaw, and in the country as a whole. It was necessary to create conditions almost overnight for Warsaw to serve as the country's policy-making centre in politics, the economy and administration and to establish cultural and educational institutions. Originally, existing buildings were pressed into service, adapted for new purposes. And so, the old Marian Institute of Education for Young Ladies from Noble Families was adapted by architect Kazimierz Skórewicz into the building of Parliament. Professor Czesław Przybylski adapted military barracks along Nowowiejska St. for the Ministry of Military Affairs (the buildings no longer exist). Starting from the early 1920s, however, new buildings for government departments and other institutions began to arise and by 1939 a considerable number of them, designed by the leading architects of the day (most of them professors at the Faculty of Architecture, Warsaw Polytechnic) had been erected.

Interesting projects were undertaken also in order to reduce the housing shortage. An idea of how acute this was can be derived from the book *Warsaw's Needs*, written in 1929 by someone in a position to know best: Zygmunt Słomiński, then Mayor of Warsaw: "The largest proportion of dwellings, 42 per cent, consists of one-room flats; only 12.7 per cent of flats are up to decent standards. There are flats — some 3,300 of them — with fewer windows than they have rooms. Warsaw is overcrowded to a degree unprecedented anywhere else in the world, with an average of 3.93 persons per room."

Housing cooperatives began to mushroom in Warsaw immediately after the First World War as an answer to the dramatic housing shortage. In 1921, 40 such cooperatives were operating in Warsaw, including the Warszawska Spółdzielnia Mieszkaniowa (WSM or the Warsaw Housing Cooperative) whose establishment was a milestone in the history of Polish housing cooperatives. WSM's housing estates added but a small fraction to overall housing construction in Poland, yet they constitute landmarks of town-planning, architecture and sociology. How was that done? Simply by building cheap flats accessible to the lowest-paid groups of the population, manual workers and poorly paid white collar workers. Data from 1938 show that nearly 52 per cent of WSM-built flats were 1- and 1.5-room bedsitters. So how was it that these modest flats, combined with amenities and facilities rounding out the WSM housing estates, added up to top-rank architecture which even today can be shown to foreign guests without embarrassment? Perhaps this is because WSM brought together enlightened, progressive leaders of the housing cooperative movement and the most talented avant-garde architects of that time. Their cooperation bred the success that WSM estates represent to this day.

In the last five years before the outbreak of the Second World War, Warsaw's development took off with a vengeance. After the years of the Great Crisis, which had hit Poland particularly hard, the city was enjoying an economic boom of modest proportions. That was also the time when Warsaw had for its Mayor Mr. Stefan Starzyński, a hard-working man of prodigious energy, an outstanding leader and organizer, who guided Warsaw's growth with a sure touch. Right from the start, in reorganizing the Town Hall, Starzyński called into being a new 400-strong Department of Town Planning (that is, equal in size to today's Bureau for Planning the Development of Warsaw). The Department was headed by Professor Stanisław Różański (who died recently as the Grand Old Man of Polish town-planning), the general designer of several editions of Warsaw development plans in the inter-war period. Housing construction grew apace in the years 1934—39. New thoroughfares began to cross the city. Renovation work was undertaken on a large scale. Future development was uppermost in the minds of Warsaw's leaders, however. The exhibition "Warsaw: Yesterday, Today, Tomorrow", which opened in 1938, featured among other things a map of the area where a world exhibition was to be mounted in 1945. How was anyone to know that all that would be left of Warsaw by 1945 would be 20 million metric tons of rubble?

The eminent town planner, Professor Adolf Ciborowski, has written: "The rank of capital city entails not only splendours, and political, social and cultural responsibilities, but also the possibility of danger. Over the past three thousand years, some cities have been razed to the ground precisely because they were capitals of defeated states condemned to extinction." The professor lists such capitals as Jerusalem ravaged by Nebuchadnezzar in 586 B.C., Carthage, or Tenochtitlán, the old capital of the Aztecs, on whose site the capital of today's Mexico began to grow in the 16th century. There is one special feature of the war-time destruction of Warsaw, however. Neither Nebuchadnezzar, nor those who spread salt on the ruins of Carthage, so that nothing would ever grow there again, nor finally the Spanish conquistadors, were trained architects.

Professor Helena Syrkus recalls: "In July 1939, a delegation of the Society of Polish Town-planners went to Stockholm to attend an International Congress of Modern Architecture. There, a German emigré, W. Schutto, a friend of Szymon Syrkus', told him in confidence in the presence of Stanisław Tołwiński, that a man by the name of Pabst, a Nazi, had shown him a letter of appointment as the Chief Architect of Warsaw, the post to be assumed on 1 October 1939."

We know that Friedrich Pabst's acceptance of the appointment was the first step on a road which soon brought him before his Maker. Pabst had no way of knowing that, however. It was only in the third year of the war that Nazis coined the term *Banditengebiet* or *Warschau Banditengebiet*. So, four years of ugly "creativity" were still ahead of Pabst, before he was mown down in December 1943 on the threshold of his studio in Daniłowiczowska Street by bullets from a Sten submachine gun. For the time being, it is still September 1939: the war which was to end with the blinding flash of Hiroshima, was still gathering speed. When General Czuma and Mayor Starzyński organized, or rather improvised the defence of Warsaw using the old forts from the 1880s, and earthworks hurriedly dug up by the people, Goebbels' propaganda slogan — *Festung Warschau* — had already been put into circulation. Among the people trapped in that "fortress" was the American film-maker Julien Bryan. His camera at the ready he criss-crossed Warsaw during its siege, recording images of the city, its inhabitants and army fighting to repulse the invaders. On that basis he produced a documentary film, and a shattering book of reportage, *Siege*, published in America in the early spring of 1940, in order to tell the world precisely what was in store for it if the Nazis won. Warsaw cast her spell on Bryan, too. After the war, he visited Poland repeatedly, for the last time in 1974, when he turned over to the Polish film archives his films and stock shot in Poland. He fully deserves to have a Warsaw street named after him.

Every day of the September 1939 siege of Warsaw, Mayor Starzyński, then serving as the Civilian Commissioner for the City's Defence, addressed Varsovians on the radio. I am one of the Varsovians of the older generation who remember those speeches very well. On 23 September the Mayor spoke for the last time. That speech was really his testament: "I wanted Warsaw to be great. I believed it would be great. Together with my colleagues, we charted maps and sketched the great Warsaw of the future. And Warsaw is great, much sooner than expected. Not in fifty years' time, nor in a hundred years' time, but it is today that I see Warsaw as great. As I speak to you, I can see her from the window in all her greatness and glory, enveloped in smoke and flames, the magnificent, indestructible, great fighting Warsaw. True, there is nothing but ruins where luxurious orphanages were to have stood; barricades have sprung up where gardens were to have been planted; our libraries and hospitals are ablaze — and yet it is today and not in fifty or a hundred years' time that Warsaw fighting in the defence of Poland's honour is at the pinnacle of her greatness and glory." It was his last radio speech. On that day, the power station was hit and there was no more electricity. There was no water, either. Food supplies were running out. Ammunition was running short. There were some 40,000 injured in Warsaw hospitals. Warsaw stood alone, abandoned by the disloyal allies who confined themselves to leaflets raids on German towns. Under these ·

circumstances, Warsaw was forced to surrender. Some 30,000 Varsovians had been killed, 12.5 per cent of all buildings lay in ruins. In the autumn of 1939 very many people were convinced that the end of the world had come. And yet, it was but a modest beginning of the nightmare that was yet to be visited on them.

Dr. Hans Frank, the former Minister of Justice in the Third Reich, was appointed Governor-General of the occupied Polish territory in October 1939. He kept a diary, mindful that the future historians of the Third Reich would need a source of information on the establishment of the "new order" in the East. Fate decreed a more appropriate role for it: the 30 volumes of the diary served as the main body of evidence during the trial before the International Military Tribunal in Nuremberg which sentenced the war criminal Hans Frank to death and had him executed.

The early volumes of the diary contain two entries concerning the Führer's designs regarding the future of Poland. One was entered as early as 4 October 1939: "The Führer discussed the general situation with the Governor-General and approved his work in Poland, particularly the destruction of the Castle in Warsaw, the decision not to rebuild Warsaw and the shipment of works of art out of the country." And indeed: Wehrmacht sappers were already beginning to drill holes for dynamite in the walls of the Royal Castle. Ultimately, there were 10,000 of them. At the same time, Nazi art historians — including Hans Posse, Dagobert Frey and Joseph Muhlmann — started looting works of art... The Führer's thoughts concerning the future of Warsaw were noted by Frank again ten months later, on 12 July 1940: "As for Warsaw, the Führer resolved that there was no question of rebuilding Warsaw as a Polish metropolis. The Führer wants Warsaw to be reduced, as part of general development, to the rank of a provincial town." Now, how do you reduce a capital city of over 1,300,000 inhabitants to a provincial town? But then, what are experts for? It was not for nothing that town planner Friedrich Pabst had been appointed Chief Architect of Warsaw almost three months before the German battleship Schleswig-Holstein opened fire on the Polish fort of Westerplatte, touching off the Second World War.

Soon after the occupation of Warsaw, the building of the former Technical Department of the Warsaw local authority in Daniłowiczowska Street was taken over by the German *Bauamt* (Building Department). Its offices were sealed off and some secret work was conducted within. The building was heavily guarded, but the secret soon leaked out. Maps of Warsaw were spread on drawing boards and pinned up on the walls of several rooms, alongside studies and designs showing the town as it would look in the future. The town's area and population were to be reduced ten times. Warsaw was to be inhabited by 130,000 Germans. Apart from the railway system and the three existing bridges, the plans took no account of the existing structure and layout of Warsaw. A special area was delineated on the Eastern bank of the Vistula for Poles, meant to perform slave-like duties. By a quirk of history, the plan survived the war. It was found in January 1945 in Hans Frank's office in the Wawel Castle in Cracow, containing the full set of 15 charts outlining the whole town-planning project (they are now in the archive of the Main Commission for the Investigation of Nazi Crimes in Poland). Its official title is *Warschau — die neue Deutsche Stadt*, but it is commonly known as the Pabst plan. The portfolio containing the 15 charts bears the following dedication:

"This work was carried out by the municipal planners of Wurzburg, to whom the Führer, on 20 June 1939, expressed his appreciation for their design of the town of Wurzburg. I wish to extend my thanks to my colleagues for their work which I pass on to the Governor-General of the occupied Polish territories, Minister of the Reich, parteigenosse, Dr. Hans Frank.

Warsaw, 6 February 1940."

Mayor
Dr. Dengel

Chart No. 13 — the most shocking of the lot — shows the "stages of the project": *Des Abbau der Polenstadt und der Aufbau der Deutschen Stadt*. Here is an example. In the autumn of 1940, the Nazis set out the perimeter of the district set aside solely for Jews — in other words, the ghetto. About half a million people were herded into that area of some 4 square kilometres. Starvation and epidemics decimated the ghetto population. In the summer of 1942, during the first *grossaktion*, over 32,000 Jews were transported to the extermination camp in Treblinka and its gas chambers (it was then, on 5 August 1942, that a group of children from an orphanage, led by Dr. Janusz Korczak, appeared on the so-called *Umschlagplatz*, a railway siding in the Stawki neighbourhood. Like everyone else, they were herded into chlorine-splashed cattle-wagons. The train left for Treblinka). By early 1943, only some 60,000 people working in factories serving the German war effort were left in the ghetto. On 16 February 1943, Himmler ordered the final liquidation of the Jewish quarter in Warsaw. A photocopy of that order can be seen today in the Historical Museum of Warsaw. It reads in part: "That area for *untermenschen*, which in any case would never be fit for habitation by Germans, must be razed to the ground. As for the million-strong Warsaw, a permanent and dangerous hotbed of decadence and rebellion, it must be reduced in area."

On 19 April 1943, on the eve of the Führer's birthday, SS units entered the ghetto to send its remaining inhabitants off to the gas chambers. This time, however, they found the going hard. The ghetto, supported by Polish underground Resistance organizations, rose up in arms. The heroic struggle went on for a month. Finally, on 16 May 1943, Commander of the *grossaktion*, SS Brigadeführer Jürgen Stroop, who on occasion went in for spectacular effects, personally pressed the detonator, blowing up the Warsaw synagogue amid fire and smoke. The very same day, a long and carefully prepared report was sent to Berlin, with these words embossed in schwabacher type on the cover: *Es gibt keinen jüdischen Wohnbezirk in Warschau mehr!* And again, by an irony of fate, the Stroop report survived the war, in two copies in fact, to serve as evidence at that war criminal's trial. Now that the ghetto was empty, German demolition teams could begin unobstructed to clear it of ruins.

Professor Jan Zachwatowicz, an architect himself, who was one of the few people to take an illegal peek at the Pabst plan during the war, has written: "When in the years 1943—44, after the ghetto had been emptied of people and burnt down, I observed demolition of every house in the area (seemingly absurd in war-time and given the situation on the front), I realized that the demolition squads were working to a plan. The gutting and demolition of the remaining districts following the defeat of the Warsaw Rising, was also part of the same plan."

It is the town planner's privilege that he, ahead of everyone else, knows what the town he works for will look like in the future. He charts that vista and contributes to its realization. But take Friedrich Pabst, an architect and town planner from the beautiful Wurzburg am Main. What was he thinking, strolling along Warsaw streets in April 1943, when a column of dark smoke rose above the ghetto, and later, in the autumn of 1943, when trainloads upon trainloads of brick were taken out of the murdered district, which "would in any case never be fit for habitation by Germans"? After all, the area was being cleared for the construction of the first districts of the *neue Deutsche Stadt Warschau* for 130,000 Germans, which he and his team had designed.

Let no-one say, "He received an order and had to execute it". Let no-one say that. It would be an over-simplification, as is shown by the behaviour of Dr. Wilhelm Hagen, a German physician who — when it came to the crunch — took the risk of being, first and foremost, a human being. His attitude was described in the book *Okupacyjne dzieje samorządu Warszawy* (Warsaw's Self-government under the Occupation) by Henryk Pawłowicz, then the Polish Deputy Mayor of Warsaw. He describes Hagen as "one of the most decent Germans in the town authorities... a true physician in every sense of the word, intense and self-controlled, with no anti-Polish chip on his shoulder. He genuinely wanted to help the Polish physicians... Dr. Hagen was one of very few Germans who had the courage to oppose the official line. When he learnt about the tragedy of the Zamość children, he publicly condemned the Nazis' action and authorized Mr. Starczewski to go where the children had been taken to see whether the Municipal Office could do anything to ease their suffering. Following that, Dr. Hagen was recalled from his post and sent to the front." To the Eastern front, let us add; in February 1943, soon after the Stalingrad debacle, that was heavy punishment... According to available information, Dr. Hagen came out of the war alive, and took up his medical practice in the Federal Republic of Germany. We do not know whether he is still alive, but Warsaw has retained his name in grateful memory.

Right from the start, from the first days of the occupation, Warsaw began to lead two lives: the official one (which Varsovians called "make-believe life"), and life in the underground, obviously in defiance of the occupying forces. Things may have looked almost the same in all the capitals of occupied European countries, but not quite. Alongside spontaneous resistance and meticulously organized armed struggle — subversion, sabotage, intelligence, etc. — clandestine secondary schools and universities continued the work of prewar educational institutions. Research was conducted, poetry written and published, music composed. Under regulations passed by the occupying authorities, "every German policeman" had "the right to shoot every passer-by in the street if he seemed suspect". And yet, not one area of Warsaw's life was suspended during the war. Through all those years, Warsaw town planners, too, kept very busy. They formed several groups, of which the most active was the Architectural and Town planning Workshop, affiliating former housing cooperative leaders, architects from WSM (Warsaw Housing Cooperative) and the Society of Working-class Housing Estates. Even as Pabst and his people were slaving over the insane plan to reduce Warsaw to the rank of a provincial German town, Polish town planners were hard at work on studies into the development of Warsaw and the surrounding region. Many of the architects who stood at the drawing boards in clandestine studios did not live to see the end of the war and to put their plans and designs into practice. Nor did anyone know then what fate was in store for the city. But now the moment of liberation was fast approaching. On 1 August 1944, the Warsaw Rising broke out. 63 days of struggle fought by Warsaw in the summer of 1944 constitute one of the most heroic, and at once most tragic, chapters of Warsaw's history. On 5 August 1944, Hans Frank noted in his diary: "Most of Warsaw is in flames. Burning the houses down is the most effective way of depriving the insurgents of their hideouts. After the rising has been suppressed, Warsaw will meet the fate it deserves. It will be totally demolished and razed without a trace."

At least 250,000 Varsovians were killed during the 63 days of the Rising, fought with a fury sometimes compared to that of the fighting in Stalingrad. The city had been turned to rubble. The stage was set for the final act of Warsaw's holocaust. After the insurrectionists had surrendered and the remaining population had been driven out, in the autumn and winter of 1944, *Vernichtungskommando* units entered the city. Using flame-throwers, dynamite and bulldozers, they went methodically from one house to another and blew up whatever was still left standing. The final tally of the results of the Nazi occupation of Warsaw was this: 850,000 Varsovians killed or murdered (i.e. two-thirds of the prewar population as of 1 September 1939); 85 per cent of Warsaw's buildings and technical facilities destroyed. During one of his last public speeches in the Reichstag, Hitler said with evident satisfaction that Warsaw was no more than a name on the map of Europe.

On 17 January 1945, Warsaw was liberated by units of the First Polish Army, forming part of the First Byelorussian Front. A fortnight earlier, the National Home Council, during its fourth session in Lublin, had unanimously voted to reconstruct Warsaw. Since no information was available on the extent of Warsaw's destruction and the resources needed for the reconstruction job, a group of architects (called, in military fashion, "an operational group") was sent into the capital immediately after its liberation. The group was headed by Captain Józef Sigalin, an architect in civilian life. Sigalin's notes from that reconnaissance mission make shattering reading. Still, given the fact that Sigalin and all members of his group were Warsaw architects, it is little wonder that his concluding words were: "Warsaw not only should be, but indeed can be reconstructed. Despite everything, Warsaw lives, now and forever." One of the group was Professor Lech Niemojewski, then President of the Association of Polish Architects. He appealed to Polish architects to join in the reconstruction of the capital.

At that time, 162,000 people inhabited the Praga district on the Eastern bank of the Vistula, which had been liberated earlier, in September 1944. On 1 February 1945, the Council of Ministers held its first session in Warsaw. Varsovians began to make their way back to their city. They could hardly imagine a life elsewhere. Their return was not really quite legal at first. Sappers of the First Polish Army had asked the municipal authorities for time to clear the city of mines and unexploded shells and bombs. During that time, the city was to be closed to outsiders. The sappers were given the minimum time possible — six weeks. But was it possible to close the city to people driven by longing, who had walked several hundred kilometres, braving severe frost and blizzards, to return to their city? Certainly not. That exceptional situation was well understood both by the sappers and by the civilian authorities (the first Mayor of newly liberated Warsaw was Colonel Marian Spychalski, also an architect by training). So, as usual in Warsaw, the informal procedure was followed. Everybody turned a blind eye to the returning Varsovians, and by the time the Commander of the Second Warsaw Sapper Brigade reported on 10 March (i.e. right on schedule) that Warsaw was free of mines (some 60,000 duds and nearly 35,000 mines had been removed or blown up), the city's population stood at some 240,000. As the authorities was taking the decision to shift the seat of government to Warsaw, Varsovians were also clear in their minds that they wanted to return to their city immediately. The two simultaneous decisions lie at the root of the unquestionable success that is the reconstruction of Warsaw.

On 14 February 1945, the Office for the Reconstruction of the Capital was established. Just three weeks later, Mr. Zygmunt Skibniewski, deputy head of the Town Planning Department, attended a session of the Presidium of the National Home Council to introduce the first outline of the plan for the reconstruction of Warsaw. That event has attracted little attention among the capital's historians, but for Professor Skibniewski it was a memorable day, nonetheless. As he tells it, he was walking along a Praga street on his way to the building of the National Home Council when he was caught by the last air raid on Warsaw. Luckily, Polish and Soviet anti-aircraft batteries chased away Luftwaffe planes sent to bomb the Warsaw railway system before they could do any damage.

The next edition of the plan of Warsaw was completed in the spring of 1946. It was displayed at the exhibition "Warsaw Lives Again" opened in May 1946 at the Library of Congress in Washington. In his introduction to the catalogue of the exhibition, the distinguished American sociologist and town planner, Lewis Mumford, wrote that Warsaw would live again more magnificent than ever before, because she now faced ruins and misery with bravery equal to that with which she had once faced danger and death. It is that spirit, wrote Mumford, that makes Warsaw as indestructible as Athens in its time.

Mumford's prophecy has come true. Warsaw is more magnificent than ever before. Despite all the errors, mistakes and deviations of the past four decades, it is a city of rare beauty. Some say that given the scale of war-time destruction, Warsaw could have been rebuilt from scratch as a much more modern and easily habitable town than it actually is today. I think they are wrong. Warsaw was rebuilt with a view to meeting the crying needs of the first postwar years. People were returning to the ruins and they urgently needed dwellings, jobs, shops, transport — in short, everything. We could not afford the luxury of waiting for things to get better before the task of reconstructing Warsaw could be undertaken. So, we got on with the job as best we could. And now, forty years later, Warsaw is again a normal town: a modern industrial centre (Poland's second largest, after Silesia), a major seat of learning and a ranking cultural centre on the map of Europe.

If a middle-aged Varsovian, now entering the autumn of his life, were asked about the successes of the first years of reconstruction, he would probably name three: greenery, reconstruction of historic monuments and construction of the East-West thoroughfare.

Greenery: the proportion of green areas to the toal area of the city. Remember the "airing corridors" from the beginnings of town-planning in Warsaw? Long before "protection of the natural environment" became the battle-cry of ecologists, we protected Warsaw against the rapaciousness of new constructions. A system for getting fresh air to the centre of the city, with the Vistula as a natural "airing corridor", was developed. Since the war, the area of Warsaw has been extended fourfold: from 124.6 square kilometres in 1939, to 486 square kilometres today. In consequence, there are almost twenty square metres of greenery for every Varsovian. And that is quite a lot.

Historic monuments: Varsovians came to a decision that the city's historic areas would be rebuilt immediately after Warsaw's liberation. Yes, it was a way of protesting against the barbarous destruction of the city by an enemy as methodical in razing it to the ground as in everything else. The Old and New Town complex was rebuilt by the Workers' Housing Estates Enterprise (Zakład Osiedli Robotniczych, ZOR) as precisely a housing estate with a denser than usual network of shops, restaurants and bars, as well as cultural institutions (museums, galleries, headquarters of artists' unions). Blueprints used in the reconstruction of the complex were based on drawings made before the war by undergraduates at the Polish Architecture Department, Warsaw Polytechnic, headed by Professor Oskar Sosnowski. Professor Sosnowski was killed during the Nazi siege of Warsaw in September 1939, but the drawings survived. They were spirited out of Warsaw before the final defeat of the Warsaw Rising and carefully preserved, to perform a priceless service after the war as the basis for blueprints making possible the reconstruction of the historic quarters of Warsaw.

During reconstruction work, bits of old stonework were painstakingly dug up from the ruins, as if from archaeological excavations, and restored to their original places in the rebuilt buildings. The many churches and church buildings of the Old Town, as well as the mediaeval defence walls, have been rebuilt.

Even before work on the Old Town began, renovators had got to work on the "Royal Tract", the streets Krakowskie Przedmieście, Nowy Świat and Aleje Ujazdowskie.

Speaking in the French Parliament when he was Minister of Culture, André Malraux justified the need for amendments to the Protection of Historic Monuments Act by saying in part: "Even though we may be guided by the best intentions, let us not permit the destruction of the old streets of Avignon, when Poland is reconstructing every stone of Warsaw's oldest square." The operative word here is "reconstruct", and indeed there is a controversy as to whether what had been done in Warsaw has been "renovation" of historic monuments, or in fact their reconstruction from the beginning. Those doubts could be regarded as settled when in 1980 UNESCO included the Old Town of Warsaw in its World Heritage List.

In the 1960s work started in earnest on two more historic monuments of outstanding value: the palaces in the Łazienki Park and in Wilanów. The outer shell of the Łazienki Palace survived, though it had been drilled full of holes where dynamite was to be placed to blow up the palace. It is not clear why that never happened; most probably, the Nazi *Kulturträger* simply ran out of time. Inside, the palace had been gutted. Work on its reconstruction began immediately after the war, and was completed in 1965. The Wilanów complex had suffered some destruction but fortunately it had not shared the fate of most of Warsaw's other historic monuments which were simply blown up sky high. Still, it was in a sorry state. Renovation work done in the 19th century, and partly also in the interwar years, had been conducted on a piecemeal basis, with insufficient skill and thoroughness. The war, obviously, did nothing to improve the situation. In January 1945, the State took over the Palace and turned it into a branch of the National Museum in Warsaw. Professor Stanisław Lorentz, the then director of the Museum, wrote on the subject: "We were fully aware that the Museum was gaining a fine historic complex, but at the same time that it would have the difficult and responsible duty of preserving and renovating the Palace, its equipment, works of art, and outbuildings, as well as reconstructing the surrounding park." Following a decision by the Polish Cabinet of December 1954, a general reconstruction project was initiated in Wilanów, encompassing the palace itself, the grounds and the surrounding buildings. The objective was to put a stop to the deterioration of the palace, improve its technical standards and adapt it to modern requirements. The project was completed in 1965, just in time to serve as General de Gaulle's residence during his visit to Poland (it is one of the palace's functions today to serve as the residence of the most illustrious guests of the Polish nation).

1971 saw the initiation of another reconstruction project, the one Varsovians had, in their heart of hearts, awaited with greatest anticipation. Professor Adolf Ciborowski has written: "There are few buildings, and probably not one built anywhere in the world within the last thirty years, which are the focus of such emotions and widespread national interest as the Royal Castle in Warsaw, now being rebuilt." Varsovians do not like ostentation, or displays of emotion and cover them up with ridicule, pretended cynicism, a mask of indifference. And yet, I well remember the day in July 1974, when the cupola was lifted onto one of the towers. There was a crowd of people in the Castle Square. I was among them with my heart in my mouth; many of the people around me reached for their handkerchiefs with suspicious regularity.

The Royal Castle has been restored to its former splendour. So has the Ujazdów Palace, another royal residence. That does not mean, however, that the renovators' work in Warsaw is finished. Whole areas of Warsaw built at the turn of the century and early in the 20th century, such as the City Centre, Wola or Praga, await their attention. For long years, we looked down on that type of architecture as petty bourgeois, and treated it with disdain. During repairs, 19th-century decorations were knocked off with abandon. It was only when the age of prefab buildings dawned, with its unrelenting monotony of straight lines, that we learnt to appreciate the beauty not only of Art Nouveau, but also of other early 20th-century aesthetic trends. There was a period of transition when we were still unconvinced, but already started treating the architecture of that period as some moving piece of bric-à-brac left over from granny's time. In the end, we realized how valuable all the construction from that period was, and that utmost care should be taken to preserve and modernize those areas so that they become fully-fledged parts of contemporary Warsaw.

Soon after the end of the war, the Poniatowski Bridge across the Vistula was rebuilt, linking the Eastern and Western parts of Warsaw. At that time, most people lived on the Eastern bank and crossed the river daily to work on construction sites on the Western side. So, in 1947 the decision was taken that another bridge should be thrown across the river to ease this large-scale movement of people. Seemingly, the decision was easy: the piers of an old bridge, the Kierbedź bridge, were left standing, so all that was necessary was to link them by building new spans on top of them. The Pancer viaduct linking the bridge to the city lacked only two spans, which had been blown up by the *Vernichtungskommando*. The decision to proceed was all but taken when a new suggestion came up, calling for the construction of a whole new East-West Thoroughfare. One of its designers recalled years later: "I don't know which was more shocking: the extent of demolition needed to build the thoroughfare, or the proposed deadline for its completion — just two years. No wonder that the Ministry of Transport, then responsible for road designs, turned down the project and the proposed schedule." It took a personal decision by the country's President, Mr. Bolesław Bierut, on 4 July 1947, for the proposal to be accepted. The magnitude of the project was breathtaking:

within 22 months, a 7-kilometre thoroughfare was to be built, including a 200-metre tunnel and a new bridge, and on top of that — a brand-new housing estate, Mariensztat; also, a dozen or so historic monuments were to be renovated. It is hard to describe the joy with which Varsovians greeted the commissioning of the thoroughfare right on schedule, on Poland's National Day, 22 July 1949. Crowds from all over Warsaw, indeed from all over Poland, flocked to Mariensztat Square in order to see that marvellous island of happiness in the midst of ruins. The importance of that moment cannot be exaggerated. Even the greatest sceptics came to believe that the generation which witnessed the war-time destruction of Warsaw, would live to see it rise from the ashes and live again.

Today people turn their noses up at Mariensztat; that marvel of postwar reconstruction is now no more than an ordinary housing estate. Young people wanting to speed in their baby Fiats as if they were Formula One racing cars complain that the East-West Thoroughfare is cramped and narrow. Little do they care that to begin with the thoroughfare's builders had one, just one, excavator, dubbed Michał, after the then Minister of Reconstruction, Professor Michał Kaczorowski. In their youth, today's grandfathers saw their city in ruins. Then they danced in the Mariensztat Market Square, helped build housing estates mushrooming all over the town, and sang the song about Antek, the bricklayer, who loved Warsaw so much that he lost the love of his sweetheart, Fela. It would be unreasonable, perhaps, to expect the younger generations to become excited about the things which today's grandfathers cared about so deeply. And yet maybe that is not totally impossible. A new construction project, first mooted as long ago as 1916, and then discussed all through the interwar years, has got under way: the construction of the Warsaw Underground. In fact they did more than talk before the war. Under Stefan Starzyński, geological studies were begun where the first projected line of the underground was to run. In the 1950s, construction of the first line, planned to go deep underground, actually began, but ran into insurmountable geological difficulties. Construction of the underground was constantly postponed as more urgent tasks demanded priority. Finally, in the autumn of 1982, the roar of Polish-made "Waryński" excavators began to be heard in a Southern area of Warsaw. Construction of the underground, to run just below street level, had finally begun in earnest. In about 10 years' time, the first line — cutting right across the city from South to North — should be in operation.

Another area where no-one should expect the generation of today to become excited about postwar gains is housing construction. And yet, any comparison between the situation today and that of prewar times would seem to point to unquestionable success. We have already mentioned the report *Warsaw's Needs* by City Mayor, Zygmunt Słomiński, which showed that in 1929 there were an average of 3.93 persons for every room; today the figure is 1.08. The difference is obvious, but today's young people, born decades after the war, look at it differently. The fact that before the war we came near to topping the European overcrowding league cuts little ice with them. They want flats, and not just any flats. The Warsaw Housing Cooperative with its prewar one-room-and-a-half flats would probably go bankrupt today. And who is to blame them? They are obviously right, and that is why housing shortage has been accorded top priority in contemporary Warsaw.

Everyone concurs that this should be so, from the Deputy Mayor of Warsaw in charge of housing construction, through harassed chairmen of housing cooperatives who have crowds of young Varsovians from the various postwar baby booms milling outside their office doors, to the proverbial mother-in-law who looked forward to peace and quiet in her retirement, but has to accept that her son-in-law will move in, that she will be the one to look after the grandchildren. It matters little that the young man's parents started depositing money for his flat twenty years ago, almost the day he was born. His housing cooperative notified him in its last letter that his application would not be considered before 1986.

So, housing construction is certainly uppermost in Varsovians' minds. Much more housing must be built. Also, much more care and effort should be devoted to ensure a high quality finish to blocks of flats and estates built in Warsaw, well... not really built, in fact, but assembled on the construction site from huge prefab elements. This technology has few enthusiasts and makes for monotony and sameness in large areas of the town. Still, truth to tell, the designers of Northern Ursynów led by Marek Budzyński have used the technology much more ingeniously to create more attractive blocks of flats than the designers of surrounding estates. In fact, the technology consigns the very word "housing estate" to history, as the estates of today differ in every respect from what went under this name in the town planning of the past.

My library of Varsaviana includes one book to which I return particularly often and on various occasions: *Cztery wieki poezji o Warszawie* (Four Centuries of Verse about Warsaw), an anthology compiled, and with an introduction by Juliusz W. Gomulicki. It is amazing that generation after generation of poets waxed lyrical about Warsaw in a highly emotional way. Jan Kochanowski devoted epigrams to the first bridge built by King Sigismund Augustus ("Here is a happy shore..."); in our times, Władysław Broniewski declared: "There is a town on the Vistula, more beautiful than our death." What can explain so much admiration for the medium-sized, not particularly attractive town on the Mazowsze plain, strung out along a broad, but grey, lazily flowing river? Poets have it in them to extol the object of their feelings to the sky. But take the words of that great sage, Władysław Tatarkiewicz, a professor at three universities, philosopher, aesthetician and historian: "Warsaw is my place under the sun, too. I once saw a propaganda leaflet of the Tourist Society which by means of concentric circles emanating from Warsaw sought to prove that Poland's capital was in the very centre of the civilized world. I do not think that's true. But that's where I feel Warsaw really is."

I share that feeling, and so, most certainly, do other Varsovians born and bred.

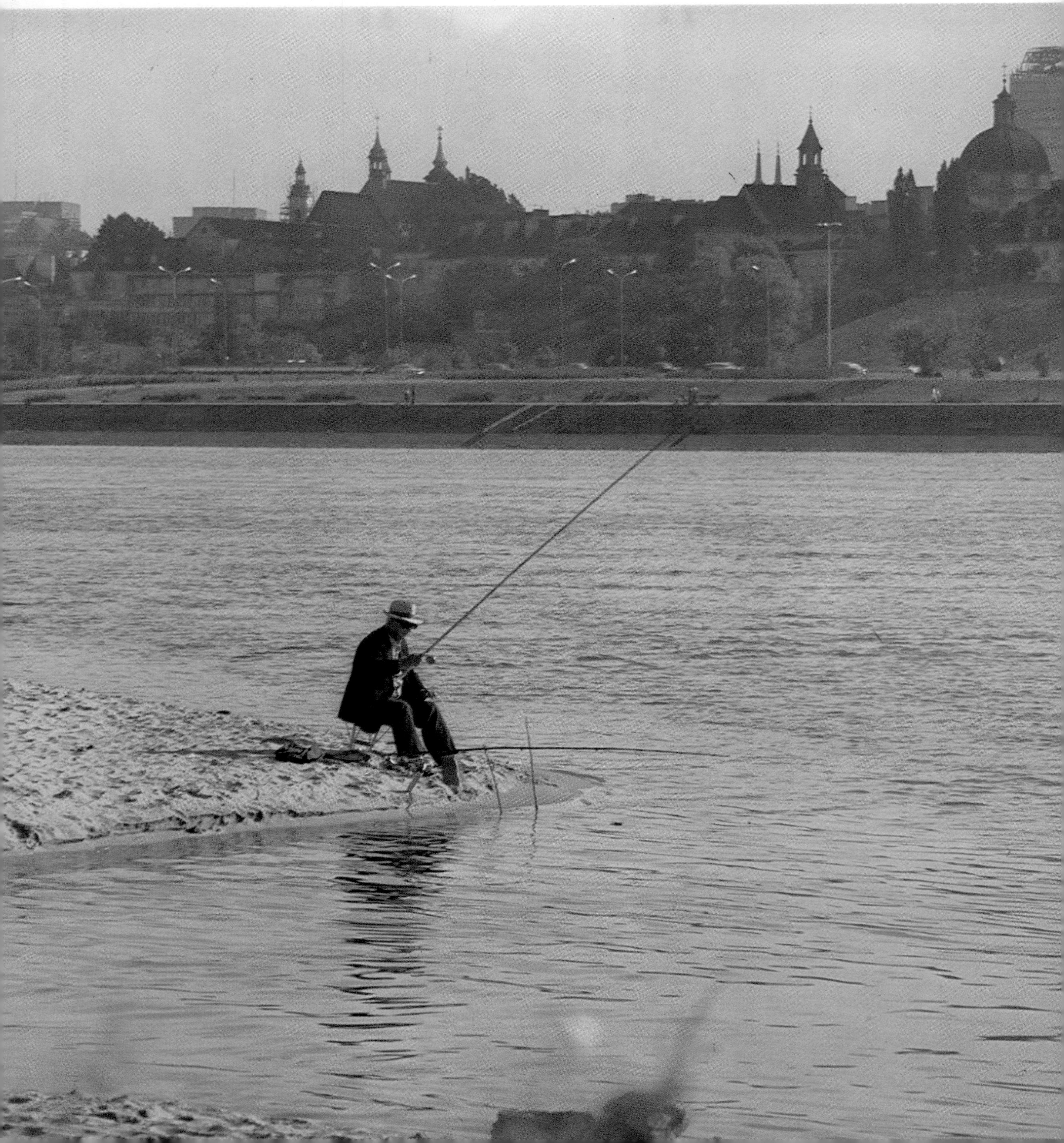

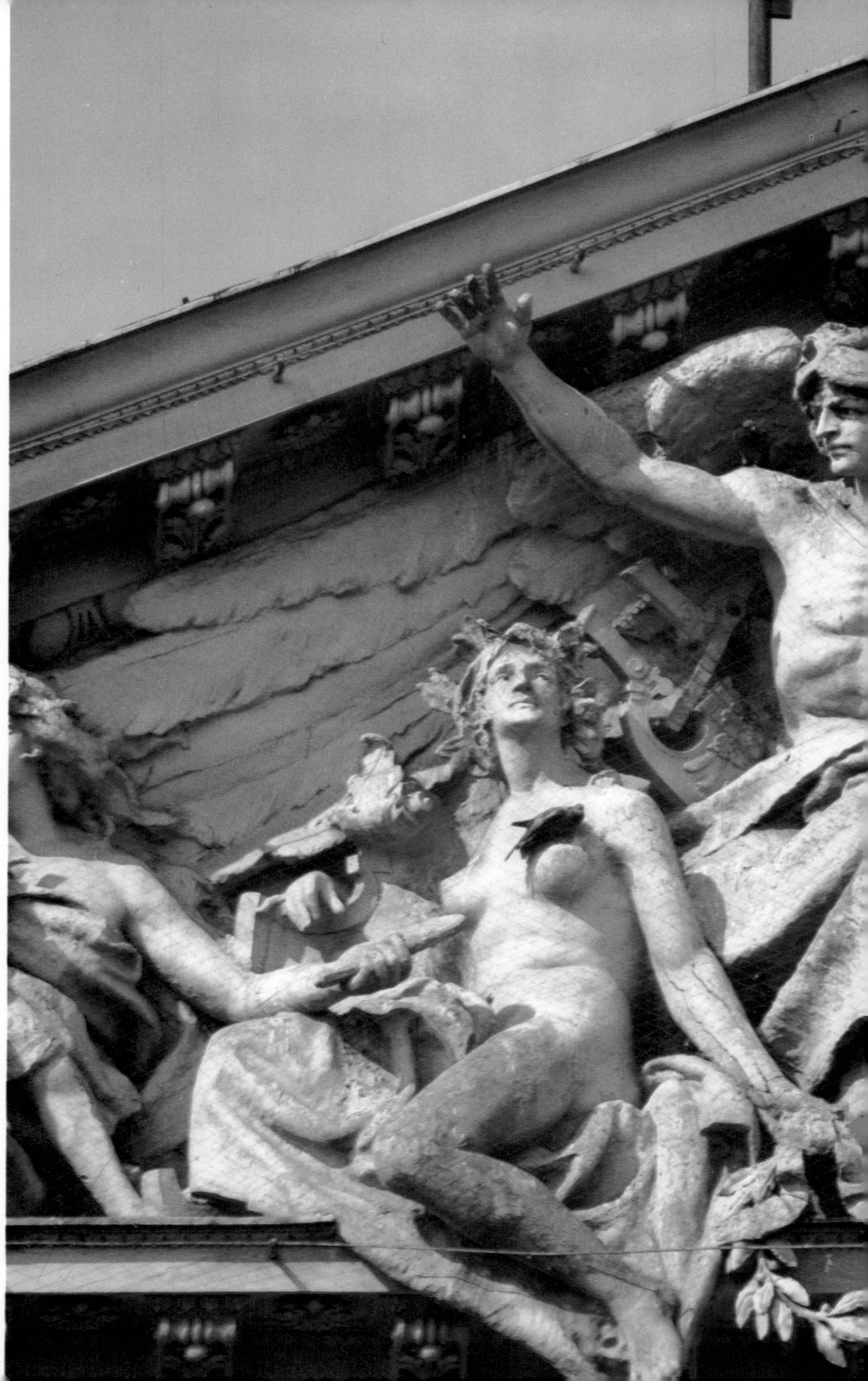

VITA
LEKARSKA SPÓŁDZIELNIA PRA
ODDZIAŁ
·VITA·
PRZYCHODNIA
LEKARSKO-DENTYSTYCZNA
WARSZAWA ul. TARGOWA 46
TEL. 19-10-63
czynna w godzinach 8-20
damski
fryzje
męski
PRACOWNI
BIELIZN
JAN TARNOWSK
w BRAMIE
WÓZK
w BRAMIE na PRAWO
SZELER i S-Ka
LEKARZY
SPECJALISTÓW

List of Illustrations

Production editor: Wiesław Pyszka

This book appears also in Polish, French, German and Russian

This is the two thousand two hundred and forty-eighth publication of Interpress

Printed in Poland